USA TODAY. TEEN WISE GUIDES

TIME, MONEY, AND RELATIONSHIPS

BUDGETING
SMARTS

How to Set Goals, Save Money, Spend Wisely, and More

SANDY DONOVAN

TWENTY-FIRST CENTURY BOOKS / MINNEAPOLIS

Twenty-First Century Books
A division of Lerner Publishing Group, Inc.
241 First Avenue North
Minneapolis, MN 55401 U.S.A.

Website address: www.lernerbooks.com

Library of Congress Cataloging-in-Publication Data

Donovan, Sandra, 1967–
     Budgeting smarts : how to set goals, save money, spend wisely, and more / by Sandy Donovan.
        p.   cm. — (USA TODAY teen wise guides: time, money, and relationships)
     Includes bibliographical references and index.
     ISBN 978–0–7613–7016–1 (lib. bdg. : alk. paper)
     1. Finance, Personal—Juvenile literature. 2. Credit—Juvenile literature. 3. Consumption (Economics)—Juvenile literature. I. Title.
     HG179.D6358 2012
     332.024—dc23   2011021553

CONTENTS

INTRODUCTION
YOU'RE THE *Boss*

It's Saturday morning, and you collect your allowance. You have no real plan for the day, but that allowance is burning a hole in your pocket. Hmm, time to head to the mall. Some sunglasses catch your eye. You don't really need them, but they're extremely cool—so you shell out the cash. Then you buy a slice of pizza, which makes you really thirsty. You check your pocket. Yep, $2 left—just enough for a beverage. Oops! *There goes your allowance.*

Spending all your allowance right away at the mall is not the greatest move. You can make better decisions when you learn to manage your money.

It's Saturday night, and your best friend texts you. Want to go see a movie? *Sweet*, you think, *that sounds great*. Except for one thing. You bought those sunglasses, and now you're broke. You have to pass up on the evening out and settle in with your parents to watch TV.

If you're like most teens, you're probably beginning to manage your own money. Hopefully you don't make mistakes such as the one described above—at least, not more than once. Because that's letting your money be the boss of you. Instead, *you need to be the boss of your money*. By learning a few tricks, you can manage your money and put it to work for you. Then it will be up to *you*—not your money—whether you stay in or go out.

1 WHY Budget?

Some teens have to work for their money, while others get big allowances from their parents. Budgeting the money you have will help you reach your goals.

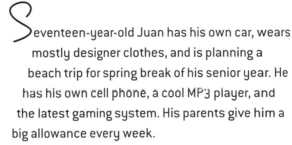

Seventeen-year-old Juan has his own car, wears mostly designer clothes, and is planning a beach trip for spring break of his senior year. He has his own cell phone, a cool MP3 player, and the latest gaming system. His parents give him a big allowance every week.

Meanwhile, Jacob's parents have trouble making ends meet. They can't afford to buy Jacob a car, a computer, or a cell phone. They don't give him an allowance, so Jacob has a job and pays for some things himself. But his weekly paycheck isn't as big as Juan's allowance.

Fast forward two years, and Juan and Jacob are both in college. One of them has an apartment near campus and spends his free time seeing local bands with friends. The other is living at his parents' house, driving an hour each way to classes. He doesn't have enough time or money to hang out with friends very often.

Sticking to a budget will help you save money for college so you can spend more time relaxing with friends and less time trying to catch up with your payments.

Think you know who's who? Would you be surprised to learn that Jacob is the one with his own apartment and a busy social life and that Juan, who seemed to have everything he wanted in high school, is still living with his parents?

BUDGETING MADE
THE DIFFERENCE

So what happened? How come the person who started out with the most money is having the biggest money problems? Well, nothing happened. But one thing made all the difference for Juan and Jacob. It's called budgeting.

Budgeting is managing your money. It's the art of making a budget—a spending and savings plan—and sticking to it.

Think of a budget like a math equation. A budget helps you make sure that the money you have coming in—from jobs, your allowance, and gifts—is equal to or greater than the money you have going out, including cash you spend on little things, cash you save to spend on big things, and money you donate to others.

JACOB'S SUCCESS

Making a budget—and sticking to it—can be the difference between achieving your goals and not achieving them. Jacob made a budget to achieve his goal of getting to college. He knew that his parents wouldn't be able to contribute money to his college expenses, so he began planning early. He figured out that he qualified for some scholarships and loans to help pay for tuition, but he knew he'd need money for books and living expenses in college.

During his junior year of high school, Jacob found a job at a grocery store, bagging customers' groceries. He worked nine hours a week, and his weekly paycheck came to $54.

Since he didn't get an allowance, Jacob was excited to have $54 every week. He thought about all the things he could do with the money: go to the movies, buy new clothes, and download music. Then he remembered he had a bigger goal: he wanted to go to college and pursue his dream of becoming a teacher. Jacob knew he'd have to forget about some of his immediate wants—like music and clothes—to achieve his longer-term goal of college.

Jacob started saving most of his paycheck. Each week he kept $14 in cash to spend and deposited the

SUMMER JOB 101:
SAVE, DON'T SPEND

By Susan Decker

Attention lifeguards and lawn cutters: Before you blow your summer earnings on CDs, consider the advantages of investing.

For high school and college students, getting a summer job [can be] easy. The hard part is figuring out a way to save some money.

A typical summer job for many teens is as a lifeguard at a local pool or mowing lawns. There's plenty of temptation to spend their pay, and many students do.

"I blow it, mostly," says Tennessee Technology University senior Chad Pierce, 24, who is working the summer as a rafting guide. "I put a little away (for college expenses), but that's what student loans are for."

Pierce isn't alone. For most students, the paycheck goes for concerts, clothes and movies. They save far less than they should, according to financial planners, educators and students themselves.

"I try to manage my money, but it seems to manage me," says Emily Johnson, 19, a junior at Northern Arizona University in Flagstaff. Johnson has two jobs— one with a temporary personnel agency and another at a concert venue.

other $40 in a bank account. He also deposited any money he got as a gift. By the end of his junior year, he had more than $1,600 in his bank account. He kept saving, and by the end of his senior year, he had almost $4,000. Once he added all the checks he received as graduation gifts, he had almost $5,000. That was enough to pay rent for his first year of college.

Paying off her credit card debt, car insurance and other expenses left only a little money to save for school expenses. To save more, she stopped using credit cards and is living at home this summer.

Budgeting is important, especially when saving for school, or for a car—the top reasons young people save. But according to a recent survey on youth and money by the American Savings Education Council, only 23% of students make a budget and stick to it. And only half of students say they always save money when they get it from work or as gifts.

"Spend 25%, if that, and save the rest," advises Simmi Mehta of San Ramon, California, who is doing clerical work and organizing kids' activities to save for her college fund. She will attend Stanford University [in California] in the fall.

She's an aggressive saver. Most experts say students should save at least half their earnings.

Saving should be done in a disciplined way. Even if your only income is from a family allowance, put aside a few dollars. When you get a summer job, the habit of saving is already there. And you won't have to go into the wilderness to avoid spending your money.

—June 25, 1999

JUAN'S STRUGGLE

Meanwhile, Juan didn't have a bank account or a job. In addition to his allowance, he got big checks from his relatives for birthdays and holidays. He usually had plenty of money to buy the things he wanted. But then he did something risky. He received a credit card offer in the mail, filled out the application, got his parents to sign it, and ordered a credit card.

When he bought things with a credit card, Juan didn't feel as if he was spending real money. He bought more clothes, he bought more games, and he started taking his girlfriend out for nice dinners—a lot. His credit card bill grew quite high, and he didn't always have the money to pay if off each month. Instead, his balance—the amount of money he owed—grew and grew. Because he didn't pay off the balance, the credit card company started charging him extra fees. By the end of his senior year of high school, he owed more than $7,000.

Juan's parents told him he would have to pay off his credit card bill before they would help him pay for college. So he got a job and lived at his parents' house so he could save money. He enrolled in two college classes, which was all he could afford. But between his job and the long commute from his parents' house, he didn't have much time to see friends. Juan told himself he was never going to let money problems hold him back again. He started learning about budgeting.

MAKE YOUR OWN BUDGET

It's never too early or too late to take control of your own money. Making a budget is the quickest way to get control. Remember: a budget helps you make sure that the money you have coming in equals or is greater than the money you have going out. It really is that simple. To get started, think about budgeting as an equation: money in minus money out.

MONEY IN

On one side of your equation is the money you have coming in. This money is your income. Income can come from a job, an allowance, or gifts. To find your monthly income, look at the past three months. Total any paychecks you earned in those three months, add any cash you

HOW TO KEEP TRACK OF YOUR BUDGET

People have many different options when it comes to budgeting. You can track your budget manually using a pen and paper or you can track it electronically using a computer. On a computer, you can make your own charts using word processing software or you can use a special software designed for household budgeting. Budgeting programs come with premade charts and worksheets. You fill in the numbers, and the software does the calculations.

earned from jobs such as babysitting, and add your allowance if you get one. Then divide that number by 3. The result is your monthly fixed income. It is the amount you typically receive in one month.

Suppose you can always count on your grandmother giving you several hundred dollars on your birthday or at Christmas. Divide this total by 12, and add it to your monthly fixed income. All this income is the "money-in" side of your budget equation.

USA TODAY Snapshots®

Kids' weekly allowance
What parents give:

- Less than $10 **29%**
- $10 to $20 **16%**
- More than $21 **9%**
- Don't give one/Other **46%**

Source: Echo Research for American Express survey of 506 households with kids ages 6 to 16.

By Anne R. Carey and Alejandro Gonzalez, USA TODAY, 2010

More than half of U.S. teens receive an allowance. Teens also get money from part-time jobs and from birthday and holiday gifts.

MONEY OUT

The second half of your budget equation consists of your expenses—or all the money you have going out. Total any fixed expenses, or payments you regularly make each month. For instance, if you pay your own cell phone bill, car insurance, or car loan, the payment is probably the same each month. Other fixed expenses might include bus fare or an Internet bill.

Some of your expenses, such as food, clothing, and entertainment purchases, will vary from month to month. You can determine these variable expenses by adding up your total spending in these areas for three months. Divide the totals by 3 to get your monthly variable expenses.

Add your fixed expenses and your variable expenses to determine your total expenses and then subtract that total from your monthly income. The amount that's left is what you have available to save for larger purchases, donate to charity, or spend on extras.

A SAMPLE BUDGET

Once you've filled in all the blanks, your monthly budget might look like this:

MONTHLY MONEY IN

ITEM	AMOUNT
Allowance	$ 56
Wages from job	$ 210
Gifts (yearly total divided by 12)	$ 25
Total monthly income	$ 291

MONTHLY MONEY OUT

ITEM	AMOUNT
Bus fare	$ 30
Cell phone bill	$ 50
Movies (one a week)	$ 40
Lunch out (once a week)	$ 32
Clothes	$ 50
Miscellaneous	$ 40
Total monthly expenses	$ 242
INCOME MINUS EXPENSES	**$ 49**

In this example, money in is greater than money out. You have almost $50 left every month to save, donate to others, or spend on extras.

But what if your money out is greater than your money in? Then it's time to make some budget changes.

2 EYES ON
the Prize

A budget can help you plan for all the things you would like to buy, like new school clothes or a new video game system.

ere's the fun part about budgeting. You get to think of all the things you want in life and then make a plan for how to achieve them. To get started, take a sheet of paper and list your goals. Don't worry if they seem unrealistic—just get them down on paper. You can include everything from "Get new soccer cleats" to "Visit Africa" to "Become president of a large company."

After you've listed some goals, you'll want to prioritize them, or figure out which ones are the most important. That decision will depend on your values. All people have values, or principles and ideas that guide them in life. For instance, some teens value animal rights. They might act on these values by not eating meat or by volunteering at an animal shelter. A teen who values friendships and relationships might go out of her way to help a friend who's having a rough time.

Look at the following list and choose five or six items that you value most. Or come up with things that aren't on the list.

Academics	Faith	Obedience
Acceptance	Fame	Organization
Admiration	Family	Peace
Appearances	Freedom	Popularity
Approval	Friendship	Power
Attention	Grades	Quiet
Authority	Happiness	Reality
Cleanliness	Hard work	Reason
Clothes	Health	Relationships
Communication	Honesty	Religion
Competition	Image	Respect
Conformity	Independence	Security
Cooperation	Integrity	Self-reliance
Creativity	Knowledge	Serenity
Education	Logic	Sincerity
Efficiency	Love	Status
Entertainment	Manners	Success
Equality	Money	

NOT ALL GOALS ARE THE SAME

Once you've identified several values that are important to you, go back to the list of goals you wrote down earlier. Go through your list and see how each goal relates to one or more of the values you identified. Cross goals off your list if they don't really relate to your values. For instance, if your values are cooperation, faith, friendship, peace, and religion and one of your goals is a $200 pair of designer

DON'T FORGET TO DONATE

Most teens have small budgets, which means that covering even basic expenses can be difficult. But remember: no matter how small your budget is, there are always people with less money than you have. Donating a part of your income each month or each year is a good way to contribute to your community. Reserving a line in your budget for donations can help you get in the habit of helping others.

Another way to donate is by giving your time, for instance, by helping out at an animal shelter.

jeans, you can pretty safely cross that goal off your list. It doesn't have anything to do with the values you identified. However, if your values include appearances and clothes, then those jeans are probably pretty important to you. Leave them on your list of goals.

Once you have a good list of goals, divide them into short-term and long-term goals. Short-term goals are those goals you want to achieve in

Many teens hope to buy their own car. That's a long-term goal and will require planning to accomplish.

the relatively near future, such as buying that new pair of jeans or scoring some decent athletic shoes before basketball season begins.

Long-term goals are those goals that will take you longer to achieve. Buying a car is a long-term goal for many teens. For others, going to college is their most important long-term goal.

MAKE A PLAN

How exactly are you going to pay for your short- and long-term goals? Unless a goal is extremely inexpensive, such as a song download, *you're going to need to save some money.* The first step is to figure out how much each

The purchasing power of teens

Spending by teens ages 13-18 totals almost $200 billion annually. Individually, teens spend nearly $7,800 a year.

Where it comes from

Money from **$5,496**
parents

$727 **$1,522**
Allowance Income
(babysitting, jobs, etc.)

Where it goes
(Top spending categories)

Clothes
Eating out
Cars
Movies
Cellphones

Source: Harrison Group

By Adrienne Lewis, USA TODAY, 2007

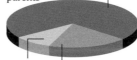

The typical U.S. teen spends more than $7,500 per year. Most of that money comes from parents.

goal will cost. Then take that price and divide it by the amount of months until you need or want to make the purchase. You can use a worksheet like this:

GOALS WORKSHEET

	COST	MONTHS UNTIL PURCHASE	MONTHLY SAVINGS NEEDED
SHORT-TERM GOALS			
Jeans	$200	4	$50
Xbox	$200	6	$33
Holiday presents	$150	3	$50
LONG-TERM GOALS			
Car	$5,000	24	$208
TOTAL MONTHLY SAVINGS NEEDED			**$341**

WANT OR NEED?

The first thing you'll notice about your Goals Worksheet is that the monthly savings total is pretty high. Remember, these savings are going to have to fit into your overall budget, which already has to cover your fixed and variable expenses.

If your monthly income is not enough to

cover your expenses plus your savings goals, you'll need to do some strategic planning. The first step is to separate your wants from your needs. You probably already know the difference between a need and a want. *A need is something you absolutely must have for survival.* A want is something you'd like to have. Maybe you *really, really, really* want it—but it's not absolutely necessary.

You might be surprised to learn how few needs you actually have. At the most basic level, people need only food, clothing, water, and shelter. But in the modern world, young people also need things like computers, bus fare or gas money, or money for school fees.

Go back to your list of expenses from chapter 1 and the goals you listed earlier in this chapter. Mark each item on the lists with an *N* for "need" or a *W* for "want." Be careful about including too many items in your "needs" list. Yes, food is a need, but that doesn't include buying a coffee every morning or going out for lunch every day. Those items belong in your "wants" list. And while it's true that clothing is a need, designer clothing is not.

THE 30-30-30-10 RULE

Some experts suggest using the 30-30-30-10 rule in budgeting. This rule says that 30 percent of your income should go toward spending, 30 percent should go toward short-term savings goals, 30 percent should go toward long-term savings goals, and 10 percent should be donated to charity.

TRIMMING AND SNIPPING, SLASHING AND BURNING

After you've identified your wants and needs, turn back to your budget. To make your "money in" equal to or greater than your "money out," you might have to do some trimming—or even some drastic slashing. Suppose you listed all your expenses and savings goals and they looked like this:

MONTHLY EXPENSES

Bus fare	$30
Cell phone bill	$50
Coffee before school	$40
Lunch out (twice a week)	$64
Movies (twice a week)	$80
Clothing	$100
Miscellaneous	$40

MONTHLY SAVINGS GOALS

Jeans	$50
Xbox	$33
Holiday presents	$50
Car	$208

TOTAL EXPENSES AND SAVINGS GOALS　　$745

Yikes! That's a grand total of $745 you need every month to pay your expenses and reach your savings goals. But if your equation looks like the one in chapter 1, with only about $290 on the "money-in" side, your budget is totally lopsided.

TEENS CONFRONT ECONOMIC REALITY;
from College to Fun, a Generation Adjusts

By Marco R. della Cava

At Drake High School, a dozen students fiddle with pencils and hair clips. One teen breaks the silence.

"I had no idea until I walked into this room today that everyone felt this was such a big issue for them," says Lindsay, 15.

A few seats away, Dani, 16, nods. "On the surface, your friends make you feel they're doing well. But I guess you see very quickly it's affecting everyone."

The elephant in this room is another big E, the economy, which for today's teens threatens to upend everything from social habits to college plans.

"The only time there are arguments in the house is when it's about money," says Caitlin, 17. "So at least now we're all talking about what we spend on which expenses, and what needs to be done to make it through this year."

Caitlin had planned to travel to Scotland with her family to visit a sister. They're assembling a care package instead. And although the senior has just been accepted to Stanford University [in California], the hit her college fund took last fall may jeopardize that dream.

Similarly, senior Jenny, 17, also has to change her college expectations from private to public, while a sister in a private university may be forced to reconsider.

For seniors, pricey prom season looms larger than ever. "I've gone since freshman year, but tickets are expensive, and then there's the limo, the shoes, the dress," says Maddi, 17. "I can see things being much lower-key this year."

With snow falling in the Sierra Nevada, Laura, 15, had visions of hitting the slopes with her family of six during February's winter break. But that Lake Tahoe trip is nixed. "We'll just stay home," she says. "It could be nice."

Staying home is the issue for Stephanie, whose relatives live in the Czech Republic. "We used to visit them every year, but now we don't know when we can go," says Stephanie, 17. "It kind of stinks, because my grandparents are old."

This teen shops at a Goodwill thrift store. Some teens shop in thrift stores instead of malls to save money.

Teens can't revive a dying investment account, but they can help take the sting out of day-to-day living. That's what drives Morgan, 17, to eschew [avoid] malls in favor of thrift shops. Or Stephanie to pass on movies with her friends and invite them over to play board games instead.

Packed lunches, part-time jobs and walking are in. Restaurants, allowances and driving are out.

"Things are a lot cozier now," Ben, 17, says with a laugh. "The standard for what makes a great weekend is a lot lower. Video games with a friend are it for me. But it's OK."

Scaling back has its psychic rewards. "This is a wake-up call to how much we had," Jenny says. "I've stopped shopping, and it feels good."

It's getting late now. Classes are over. Some kids head off to sports practices.

"We as a generation will come out of this wiser and smarter about our own financial strategies," one student says. "I'm sure of it."

Ben smiles, adding, "It's always darkest before the dawn."

Descartes? Jefferson?

"Um, no," he says. "I think it's Batman."

—*January 8, 2009*

It's time to start cutting. Do you really need those unlimited cell phone minutes or do you just want them? Do you really need coffee every day before school? What if you went out to lunch twice a month instead of twice a week? Could you buy jeans on sale instead of splurging on those $200 designer jeans?

After identifying your wants and needs, and by cutting and trimming, your new budget might look like this:

Do you need to go out with your friends for coffee every week? Maybe you could cut down the frequency to tighten your budget.

MONTHLY EXPENSES	ORIGINAL ESTIMATE	WANT OR NEED	NEW ESTIMATE	
Bus fare	$30	N	$30	
Cell phone bill	$50	W	$30	(limited minutes)
Coffee before school	$40	W	$ 0	
Lunch out	$64	W	$16	(twice a month)
Movies	$80	W	$20	(twice a month)
Clothing	$100	W	$50	
Miscellaneous	$40	W	$20	

MONTHLY SAVINGS GOALS

Jeans	$50	W	$ 0	
Xbox	$33	W	$ 0	
Holiday presents	$50	W	$25	
Car	$208	W	$100	

TOTAL EXPENSES AND SAVINGS GOALS $291

In this example, your expenses and your savings goals add up to $291—exactly the same as your income. Congratulations—your budget balances perfectly.

Cutting down the amount of minutes on your cell phone plan can help your budget.

3 TO THE *Bank*

Explore a World
OF FINANCIAL POSSIBILIT

To better manage your money, think about
opening a bank account. A bank can help you
grow your money and track your spending.

If you've followed the advice in chapters 1 and 2, you should have a good idea of your monthly budget. And if your budget includes a set amount of savings each month, you're already on the road to financial success.

It's time to put your plan into action. How are you going to make sure you're not spending too much each month and you're saving the amount you budgeted? One great tool for sticking to your budget is a bank account. Opening a bank account and using it wisely can help you keep track of both your spending and your savings. And a bank account can also help your savings grow.

BANKING BASICS

To use banks wisely, it's important to understand a little bit about them. A bank is simply a business that borrows and lends money. People and organizations often borrow money from banks, usually to make a big purchase, such as a car, a home, or a business. When people borrow from banks, they have to pay the bank interest. Interest is money that borrowers pay for the privilege of borrowing. It's usually a percentage of the amount borrowed. Banks make their money from the interest paid by borrowers.

But interest works two ways. People who borrow money pay interest, but people who put money into a bank account earn interest. When you deposit money into a bank account, you are really lending money to the bank. The bank pays you for the loan by giving you interest.

You've probably seen lots of advertisements for banks on billboards, on television, and in magazines. All those ads tell you something about banks: they want your business. They want as many customers as possible to deposit money, because while a bank is holding onto depositors' money, it can lend the money out to other people and charge them interest. The interest banks charge borrowers is much higher than the interest banks pay to depositors. That's how banks earn their money.

BANKING CAN
INCREASE YOUR MONEY

Just as banks get their money by charging interest, you can increase your money by earning interest from a bank account. The simplest kind of interest is called—you'll never guess this—simple interest. With simple interest, you earn a percentage of the money in your bank account at the end of each year.

Suppose your bank pays simple interest on your account at a rate of 4 percent. If you have $1,000 in the bank, you will earn $40 (4 percent of 1,000) at the end of your first year of saving. You'll also earn $40 at the end of your second year, your third year, and on and on. That's all you need to know about simple interest. Why? Because the other kind of interest is so much better. Once you learn about it, you'll never want to bother with simple interest.

What is this interest superstar? It's called compound interest. With compound interest, you earn interest on your interest, as well as on the original money you put into your bank account. If you deposited $1,000 into an account with 4 percent compound interest, you'd have $1,040 at the end of one year—the same as if you earned simple interest. But at the end of the second year, you'd earn $41 (4 percent of $1,040) instead of $40 in interest. At the end of the third year, you'd earn $43. Big deal, right? Actually, it is a big deal. Maybe not so much in the first year or two, but after that, *you'll start to see your money really grow.*

Say you put $100 in a savings account with a 10 percent interest rate. The following chart shows how your money would grow over fifty years with both simple and compound interest.

TIME IN BANK (IN YEARS)	SIMPLE INTEREST	COMPOUND INTEREST
1	$110	$110
2	$120	$121
3	$130	$133
4	$140	$146
5	$150	$161
10	$200	$259
20	$300	$672
30	$400	$1,744
40	$500	$4,526
50	$600	$11,739

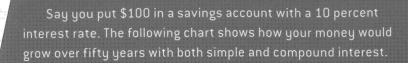

SAVINGS AND CHECKING ACCOUNTS

Banks offer many different kinds of accounts, including money market funds and certificates of deposit, but the most suitable accounts for teenagers are savings accounts and checking accounts. Savings accounts are good accounts for beginning savers because you can open an account with very little money. In most cases, if your balance (the amount of money on deposit) gets low, you won't be charged a fee. You can deposit money into the account as often as you like. You can also withdraw cash, either from the bank or from an automated teller machine (ATM).

Checking accounts are similar to savings accounts. You can open a checking account with very little money, keep a low balance,

usually without paying fees, and deposit and withdraw money as often as you like. But checking accounts allow you to write checks. Checks are pieces of paper that let you transfer money from your bank account to someone else—such as a friend, a store, or a charity.

Checks are safer than cash because they are printed with your name, which means that only you can use them. When you write a check, you must also sign your name and sometimes show identification to the payee (the person who receives the check). The payee must also sign the check and show identification to deposit the check or trade it for cash at a bank. Checks are also useful when you don't have enough cash in your wallet for those $40 jeans, but

Money business

How consumers prefer to do their banking:

- In person at branch **41%**
- Internet **24%**
- ATM **16%**
- Drive-through service at branch **17%**
- Automated or live telephone **2%**

Source: BAI online survey of 2,430 U.S. consumers. Margin of error ±2 percentage points.

By Julie Snider, USA TODAY, 2007

The transaction register that comes with your checkbook can help you keep track of each deposit and payment you make.

you do have the money in your bank account. You can write a check for the jeans instead.

KEEPING TRACK

Whether you open a savings account or a checking account, the bank will give you a small booklet called a transaction register. The booklet contains columns where you can enter every deposit or payment you make to or from your account. You can also track your banking activity with a computer program. By keeping track of your balance, you'll know whether you are spending too much, meeting your savings goals, or even exceeding your goals.

At the end of each month, your bank will send you a statement, or report, showing all the activity with your account. You can check this statement against your own records to make sure they are accurate. You can also check your bank statements and transactions online.

MORE WAYS TO BANK

In addition to checks, bank accounts give you other ways to access your cash. An ATM card looks like a credit card, but it works only at automated teller machines. With an ATM card, you punch in a personal identification number (PIN) to access your bank account. You can check your balance, withdraw cash, transfer money from one account to another, or deposit checks at an ATM.

Debit cards also look like credit cards, but they operate like checks—only faster. When you make a purchase with a debit card, you automatically transfer money from your bank account to the payee's bank account. You can use debit cards in stores, restaurants, and other businesses.

When you use an ATM card, the ATM prints out a receipt afterward. It shows how much money you deposited into or withdrew from your account. When you use a debit card at a store or other business, the clerk will also hand you a receipt. Hold onto your receipts and record them in your transaction register. Otherwise, you might lose track of your balance. You might also spend more money than you have in your account, and that can get you in trouble with your bank.

BAD BOUNCE

Checks and debit cards can make spending easier, but they can also get you in lots of trouble. If you write a check for more than the amount you have in your bank account, your check will bounce. This means the payee won't get his or her money, but you will have to pay a hefty fee—usually about $35 for each bounced check. The same thing can happen with a debit card. If you make a debit card purchase for more money than you have in your account, you might have to pay a $35 fee.

THE DOWNSIDE
TO DEBIT CARDS;
They're Convenient, but They Lack Consumer Protection of Credit

By Sandra Block

Debit cards seem to offer an ideal combination of convenience and self-discipline.

They're safer than cash and [easier] than checks. Most retailers that accept credit cards also accept debit cards. And because debit cards withdraw money directly from the card holder's bank account, they offer relief from the surprise interest rates, late fees and [complicated] terms of credit cards.

As increasing numbers of consumers are learning, however, there are drawbacks to debit cards. When it comes to fraud and theft, credit cards offer a distinct advantage over debit cards—something debit card holders may not realize until they discover that money has gone missing from their bank accounts.

In August, Erica Sandberg, 46, a journalist and credit expert who lives in San Francisco, was headed to the mall to do some back-to-school shopping for her third-grade daughter when she received a recorded phone message from Bank of America.

Consumers who use debit cards have to be careful that no one steals their card or learns their PIN.

She was told that someone had used her debit card to buy $800 in merchandise at a Dillard's department store in Phoenix [Arizona]. When she contacted the bank, a representative assured Sandberg that her account would be credited for the stolen money. Still, she didn't have access to her account for five days.

Fortunately, Sandberg's husband had his own account, and she also has a savings account she could have tapped if necessary. But she says the experience left her feeling frustrated and vulnerable, particularly since neither Bank of America nor Dillard's could tell her how the fraud occurred.

"You don't know how it happened, you don't know if it's going to happen again, and you don't even know for sure that the bank is going to believe you," she says.

[Expert advice on] protecting yourself from debit card fraud:

- Treat your debit card like cash and keep it in a safe place.
- Don't give out your card number over the phone unless you initiated the call.
- Periodically review your account, particularly if you have an online bank account. If you see discrepancies or unauthorized transactions, notify the card issuer immediately.
- Memorize your Personal Identification Number. Don't carry your PIN in your wallet or purse or write it on your ATM or debit card.
- Keep a record in a safe place separate from your cards of your account numbers, expiration dates and the telephone numbers of each card issuer so you can report a loss quickly.
- Only use your debit card at retailers you know and trust. Keep an eye on your card during the transaction, and get it back as quickly as possible.

—November 24, 2010

4 SPEND IT
Wisely

Pay attention to how you spend your money. Do you really need those expensive shoes, or would you rather have money in the bank?

Quick question: what's the single most important thing you can do to keep your budget on track? Would you be surprised to hear that it has to do with spending money and not saving money? That's right! Your spending habits can do a whole lot of good—or a whole lot of damage—to your budget.

LIVE LIKE A MILLIONAIRE

You might think of millionaires as people who drive expensive cars, wear designer clothes, and vacation all over the world. But researchers who study the habits of wealthy people have found that's not true. The fact is that millionaires are some of the thriftiest shoppers around. Among female millionaires, the most popular brand of shoe isn't superexpensive Manolo Blahnik—it's middle-of-the-road Nine West.

People with the largest bank accounts are usually the ones who don't spend a lot on clothes and restaurants. Instead, **they make do with less expensive items,** put their money in the bank, and watch it grow. Then, when they want to make a large purchase such as a house or when they run into an unexpected expense, they don't have to stress out about money.

DON'T FALL FOR THE HYPE

"But I got it on sale!" How many times have you or someone you know uttered those words after buying something expensive? Or maybe you've said, "I saved ten dollars when I bought this sweater!" The fact is, stores work hard to make you think you're saving money when you shop. But if you spend $40 on a sweater that's marked down from $100, have you really saved $60? Of course not, you've spent $40.

Don't be fooled by discounted prices you see in stores or online. Many companies price things high just so they'll be able to discount them later. So before you buy anything, look around at a few different stores and compare prices. Focus on what you're getting for your money, not on how much the store says you're "saving."

USA TODAY Snapshots®

Paying a premium

Do you consciously pay more for a luxury item at a brand store than a discount store?

$$$

Yes
59%

No
41%

Source: Accenture Consumer Luxury survey of 1,002 adults 18 and older who purchased luxury items during the holidays.

By Jae Yang and Veronica Salazar, USA TODAY, 2010

Consumers frequently pay more for fancy brand names, even though no-name brands are often just as good. To save money, look for a good deal on a no-name brand.

DON'T BE HAD BY ADS

Do your friends all like a particular brand of jeans or sneakers? Many teens—and adults—fall for brand-name hype. Is a brand-name product really better than a less expensive item? The answer is usually no, but most people think brand names are best. Why? Advertising. Companies work hard to make you want to buy their brands, and they spend a lot of money on ads to achieve this goal. Consider how many ads you see on a daily basis. You see them on television, online, in stores, in magazines, on the sides of buses, on billboards, and inside stadiums. The list is endless!

Many ads show beautiful, carefree people relaxing and enjoying the good life. Advertisers want you to believe that if you buy the product, you too will live the good life. Don't let the ads trick you. Before you buy an item, think about exactly why you want to buy it. Think back to the values and goals you identified when you made your budget. Does this item fit in with your values and your goals? If you're just buying to feel better about yourself or to impress someone else, you might want to hold off.

Companies try to get people to buy their product using beautiful advertisements. This billboard advertises an iPod.

Clipping out coupons for products you frequently buy can help save you money.

CUT COSTS WHERE YOU CAN

The key to being a smart spender isn't cutting out spending altogether. The key is knowing how to spend less and still get the benefits of spending more. Check out these ideas for keeping spending down:

- Getting together with friends for dinner and a movie? Try ordering takeout and watching a DVD at someone's house instead of going to a restaurant and a movie theater. All the fun, half the cost.
- Buy generic (nonbrand name) versions of cosmetics, drinks, and other small items. Search reviews online to find out which no-name products stack up well against brand-name items.
- Look for sales and coupons for items you buy regularly.

- Make one day each week a "spend-free" day. You may be surprised that you can survive without your daily snack, magazine, music download, or whatever else you regularly spend on.
- Take out free books, music, games, and movies from your local library.
- Hold a swap. The next time you get the urge for new clothes, music, or games, see if your friends are feeling the same way. Plan a swap meet at which you all get together to trade items. Put everything on one big pile and have each person draw a number. The person who chooses 1 gets to pick an item first, the person with 2 goes next, and so on until the pile is gone.

GO FOR LASTING QUALITY

If you resist the urge to splurge on your every want, you'll have the funds to buy the things you really need. How do you make good buying decisions?

Look for quality. Spend your money on clothing that won't rip, electronics that won't freeze up, and healthful food instead of junk food. Often quality costs extra. But most of the time, it's worth it. For instance, three pairs of quality socks, made of 100 percent wool or cotton, will probably last longer than a dozen pairs of cheap nylon socks that rip the first day you wear them.

So does that mean that you should always buy the more expensive item? Not necessarily. Suppose you're going to the beach for a week and want to buy a new swimsuit. You can get a suit for less than $20 at a discount store or you can spend nearly $100 at a department store. The department store suit is better made. The material is heavier and the stitching is stronger. The suit will probably last longer than the inexpensive suit. But you like the look of the cheap suit just as much. Should you buy the expensive suit or save the money for something else? If you think you might keep the suit for several years, it might be worth it to buy the expensive one. But think about it: do you usually wear the same swimsuit summer after summer? Or is your taste likely to change? Will you want a new suit next summer? If so, you're probably better off buying the cheaper suit.

ONLINE SHOPPING

More and more products are available online. Buying online can be a great way to get deals—but it can also be a great way to get cheated.

Before you buy anything online, compare prices. Check the item you want on several different websites to find the best deal. Many

Buying online could save you money, but make sure you are dealing with an honest seller.

sites show you store-by-store price comparisons. Some companies include a section for customer reviews on their websites. Read reviews of the products you're interested in before you decide to spend. You can also find customer reviews by typing the name of the item you want to buy and "reviews" into a search engine.

Remember that most online shopping requires a credit card, but using a credit card online can expose you to credit card fraud. Some criminals try to steal credit card numbers that people type into websites. The crooks then use the numbers to make their own purchases. Some criminals even set up fake websites that look just like real ones. When you place your order on the fake site, the site operators steal your credit card numbers as well as other personal information.

AVOID FRAUD

To avoid credit card fraud, make sure the site you're buying from is reputable. Look for seals from the Better Business Bureau (BBB) or TRUSTe, organizations that monitor businesses. *But don't be tricked.* Some crooks even put fake BBB and TRUSTe logos on their websites. If you see a logo from one of these organizations, click on it. If your click takes you to the BBB or TRUSTe home page, you'll know the site is legitimate. Also look for a closed padlock symbol in a website's address bar or on the lower right corner of the window. This symbol tells you that the site is secure from online fraud.

Many teens don't have credit cards, so you may have to ask a parent to make online purchases for you. If you do have your own credit card, you might still want to ask an adult to review your purchase to make sure you're dealing with an honest seller. Remember that you can always compare prices and gather information about a product online and then make your purchase at an actual store. Then you won't have to worry about credit card fraud.

IN-SCHOOL BANKS DISPENSE FINANCIAL SENSE:

Student-Run Sites Teach Importance of Saving, Good Credit

By Katharine Lackey

When students at Carter High School in Strawberry Plains, Tennessee, forget their lunch money, they don't have to worry about going hungry.

Instead, they wander over to one of the five tellers who work at the student-run bank, where they can withdraw money from their savings accounts or fill out short applications for a $5 loan, all without leaving the building, says Lynn Raymond, a banking and finance teacher at the school.

"We're easing them into learning about borrowing money and the responsibilities that go along with that," Raymond says of the experience students receive at the bank, which opened Feb. 16 in partnership with First Century Bank.

"It's just so important because so many people get in trouble financially," she says.

Students across the USA are increasingly getting hands-on experience about the financial sector through banks operating in high schools, and sometimes even in elementary schools.

The first in-school bank opened in 2000 in Milwaukee [Wisconsin] and today there are several dozen, says Luke Reynolds, chief of outreach and program development at the Federal Deposit Insurance Corporation.

IMPORTANT ECONOMIC LESSONS

The number of credit unions [customer-owned banks] partnering with schools is even greater; there are at least 324 credit union in-school branches that the National Credit Union Administration keeps track of.

Part of the growth in recent years can be attributed to the recession, says Karen Harris, supervising attorney for the community investment unit at Sargent Shriver National Poverty Law Center.

"If you look at what's going on with the economy, I think a lot of people have started to realize how important savings are and to develop that early," Harris says.

So far, about 65 savings accounts have been opened at Carter High School's bank and about 25 loans have been made, with 10 cents of interest due per day, Raymond says. If students forget to repay the loan, the bank sends a student worker to remind them. Students cannot have more than one loan out at a time, and if they take more than 15 days to repay the loan, their future requests for loans might be denied, she says.

For the most part, the in-school banks look like small branches often found in local supermarkets or Wal-Marts—signs designate the bank's affiliation, Harris says. Usually a representative of the bank works alongside the students, she says.

COSTS ARE NOT HIGH

The cost of opening a student-run bank is minimal for most schools, and usually all that's needed is donated space where the institution can do any necessary renovations and put in counters and equipment. Some of the schools with financial institutions:

- Charlottesville, Virginia, Albemarle High School will open an in-school credit union in fall. Students and faculty will be able to open checking and savings accounts, and students working at the branch will receive internship credit and be paid as employees of the University of Virginia Community Credit Union.
- Middletown, Delaware, Appoquinimink High School partnered with Wilmington Trust to open its student-run bank a month ago. Rebecca DePorte, senior vice president of personal financing at Wilmington Trust, says it's important to get people learning about finances when they're young. "We see what happens when people don't have that background and the challenges it can create," she says.
- Appleton, Wisconsin, Jefferson Elementary School opened an in-school credit union staffed by fifth- and sixth-graders in December, says Rick Sense, senior vice president of government and community relations at Community First Credit Union, the school's partner. So far, 125 savings accounts have been opened.

—April 1, 2010

5 TAKE Charge

Having a credit card can help build your credit history. It's important to spend only what you can afford each month.

You're probably aware of the dangers of credit cards, right? It can be all too easy to get a credit card, go on a buying spree, and find yourself hundreds or even thousands of dollars in debt—and that is *not* good for your budget.

So you should avoid credit cards like a pair of stinky socks, right? Actually, no. Although they can get you into financial hot water, using credit cards wisely can build your credit history. Having a history of good credit is critical if you ever want to rent an apartment or take out a loan for a car, a home, or another big-ticket item.

HOW CREDIT WORKS

Credit is a deal between you (the borrower) and a bank or other business (the lender). When you buy something on credit, the business lends you the money, and you pay the business back over time. Credit comes in many forms, including credit cards, car loans, college loans, and mortgages (loans for houses). Many teens get their first experience with credit by using a credit card.

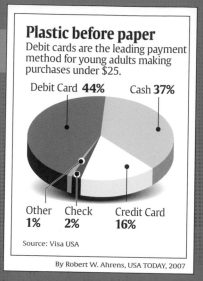

Plastic before paper
Debit cards are the leading payment method for young adults making purchases under $25.

Debit Card **44%**   Cash **37%**

Other **1%**   Check **2%**   Credit Card **16%**

Source: Visa USA

By Robert W. Ahrens, USA TODAY, 2007

For small purchases, young adults are more likely to pay with a debit card than with any other method.

When you use a credit card at a store, the credit card company pays the store right away. You pay the credit card company back in a certain period of time. What's in it for you? You get to enjoy your purchase immediately, before you've actually paid for it. What's in it for the credit card company? The company charges you interest on the amount you borrow—usually between 5 and 20 percent of the total amount. The company might also charge you fees if your payment is late or if you go over an agreed-upon credit limit.

THE TROUBLE WITH INTEREST

Whenever you take out a loan or sign up for a credit card, you agree to an interest rate. That's the extra money you pay, on top of the money you borrow to make purchases. Interest sounds pretty simple, but it can get complicated. Take a credit card with an interest rate of 15 percent. The company charges a portion of that interest each month, or twelve times a year, on the unpaid balance on your account, so each month you get charged one-twelfth of 15 percent of your unpaid balance.

Here's how it works. You make purchases throughout the month on your credit card, and at the end of the month, the company sends you a statement. The statement lists the total amount you owe and gives a minimum amount due that month. Often the minimum amount is only a small fraction of the total amount due, and you usually have twenty to thirty days to make a payment. "Cool!" you might think. "I'll just pay the $20 minimum instead of the whole $400 I owe."

But be careful—this is where you can get into trouble! If you don't pay the whole balance, the following month you get a new statement with that previous balance, any new charges, and interest for the previous balance. So if you paid $20 on a $400 balance, your statement will show that you owe $380 plus $4.75 in interest (15 percent of $380 divided by 12).

So you paid $20, but almost one-quarter of that payment went toward paying interest. If you charge another $50 on the card the next month and again pay only $20, you're going to owe more

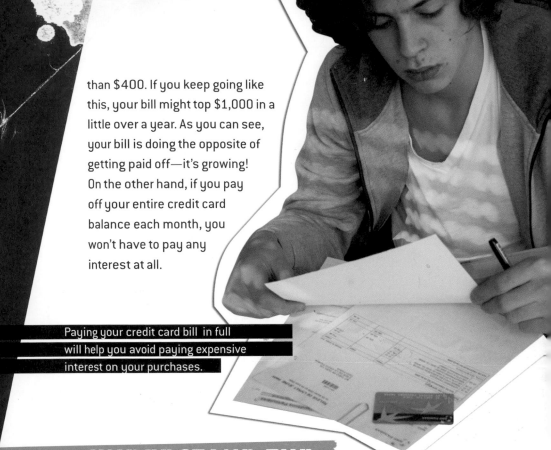

than $400. If you keep going like this, your bill might top $1,000 in a little over a year. As you can see, your bill is doing the opposite of getting paid off—it's growing! On the other hand, if you pay off your entire credit card balance each month, you won't have to pay any interest at all.

Paying your credit card bill in full will help you avoid paying expensive interest on your purchases.

UNDERSTAND THE FINE PRINT

Ever heard the expression "Read the fine print"? On credit card agreements, the print is so small that it's nearly impossible to read. Even so, carefully review the agreement before you open a credit card account. Make sure you know your annual percentage rate (APR)—the amount of interest to be charged on your unpaid balance. Be aware that many credit card companies offer an extremely low APR for one year or until you miss or are late with a payment. Then the APR may skyrocket.

Also learn about any fees the credit card company might charge you. For instance, some companies charge customers a yearly fee just

ucted
ved or it may
advance. The cost of a
generally is no grace period.
le money is withdrawn.

CARD HOLDER AGREEMENT

gives the terms and co
ement is requir
e the Annual
ula, annual fe
annual fe
include
change

Review your credit card agreement carefully.
Check the annual percentage rate and any fees
you might be charged.

to have a card—you don't want this kind of card. Most companies also charge fees if you exceed your credit limit.

UNDERSTAND YOUR CREDIT HISTORY

Your credit history is a description of all your credit activity for the past seven years or more. Lenders use this information to decide if you are responsible enough to take out another loan. Having a good credit history is critical if you ever want to buy a car or a home or sometimes even a television. Landlords and potential employers may look at your credit history. They are not giving you a loan, but they want to see how responsible you are at paying off your debts.

COLLEGE GRADS
WITH AN "A" IN CREDIT HISTORY START WITH AN ADVANTAGE

By Sandra Block

It's not unusual for college freshmen to come home for the holidays with some interesting new ideas, a few extra pounds and a couple of tattoos. But here's something most college students won't bring home this Thanksgiving: a credit card.

The credit card reform bill signed into law last year prohibits lenders from issuing cards to individuals under 21 unless they can prove they can make payments or get a parent or guardian to cosign. The provision took effect Feb. 22, 2010, so when college starts this fall, students won't be greeted by credit card issuers bearing pizza coupons and T-shirts.

The requirement is designed to prevent college students from racking up debts they can't repay. But it could also prevent them from using credit cards responsibly to build a good credit profile.

Young adults who graduate college without a positive credit history could have a hard time qualifying for a car loan, renting an apartment, even getting a job, says Gail Cunningham, spokeswoman for the National Foundation for Credit Counseling.

Even with the restrictions, parents can help college-age children build a credit history. Alternatives to consider:

- Add your child to a credit card as an authorized user. When you do this, the child can use the card, but you're responsible for the account. The card's payment history is reported to the credit bureaus in your child's name, so it will help the child build a credit record.
- Cosign a credit card for your child. This card is in your child's name, so it also helps the child build a credit history. As cosigner, you'll receive a monthly statement, and the card's credit limits can't be increased without your approval.

College students sign up for credit cards from a lender on campus. New laws require applicants under twenty-one to have a parent or a guardian as a joint signer or to prove they can make the payments.

- Find out whether your child still qualifies for a credit card. Some college students who have income from part-time jobs may be able to qualify for credit cards without a cosigner. The card may have a very low limit, but that's not a bad thing, because it limits the amount the child can spend.
- Get your child a debit card. With a debit card, you can monitor your child's spending, and replenish the account when necessary. The downside to debit cards is that they won't help your child develop a credit history. Still, if your goal is to teach your children how to handle money responsibly, having a debit card is a good first step.

—*August 17, 2010*

EPILOGUE
USE YOUR *Budget Power*

Learning to keep a budget now can help you manage your money throughout your life.

If you've made it this far, you're armed with a lot of information about how to set and keep a budget, how to save money, and how to spend wisely. You can use this knowledge to smartly manage your money—as a teen and throughout your life. Remember these quick tips for keeping control of your budget:

Tip 1: **Money in must be equal to or greater than money out.**
Your income—including your allowance, pay from jobs, and any gifts—has to cover your expenses, as well as any saving and donating you want to do. Sometimes it can be easy to spend more than you earn. For instance, credit cards easily allow you to spend more than you have, *for a time*. But you can never really be in charge of your budget and your money if your spending is more than your income.

Tip 2: **Setting goals is the key to a budget that works.**
Not knowing what your goals are is like driving to a new place without a map—you might not reach your destination. Matching your goals to your personal values will help make sure that you're going after the goals that really are important to you.

Tip 3: **Be honest about your needs and your wants.**
Advertising and other media can easily convince us that we really need things rather than simply want them. People who are in control of their budgets have figured out when to pass over some immediate wants to achieve longer-term and more important goals.

Tip 4: **Banks can help you grow your savings and track your spending.**
Banks give you a safe place to keep your money and also help you track your saving and spending. Banks offer three advantages over keeping your money in cash: safety, convenience, and interest payments.

Tip 5: **Compound interest is your friend.**
Putting your money in a savings account with compound interest is the safest way to see it grow over time.

Tip 6: **Be extremely cautious about using credit.**
Credit cards and other loans can get you into serious financial hot water—but only if you aren't smart about them. If you understand the terms of your credit and use it wisely, you can avoid spending too much, paying high interest rates, and racking up fees. And by using credit smartly as a teen, you'll build a solid credit history, which will help you get lower interest rates on loans as an adult.

Most of all, remember, when you control your money and your budget, *you can better control your life.*

GLOSSARY

ANNUAL PERCENTAGE RATE (APR): the rate of interest (expressed as a percentage) charged for a loan over a year's time

BALANCE: the amount owed on a loan or the amount of money in a bank account

BUDGET: a financial plan that lists your income and your expenses. Budgets help you track your money to reach your financial goals.

CHECK: a piece of paper one person gives to another authorizing the payment of money from the giver's bank account

CHECKING ACCOUNT: a bank account that allows you to write checks to transfer money to other people

COMPOUND INTEREST: interest paid not only on an original sum of money but also on any interest that sum earns

CREDIT: a loan of money with the expectation of future payment

CREDIT CARD: a plastic card issued by a bank, a store, or other business that allows people to make purchases and pay for them later

CREDIT HISTORY: a record of how well you've managed your credit, such as paying off loans and credit cards on time. Many businesses use your credit history to determine if they will give you new loans.

CREDIT LIMIT: the highest amount you may charge on a credit card. The company that issues the credit card sets the limit.

DEBIT CARD: a plastic card that allows you to make purchases at stores and other businesses. When you pay with a debit card, the money electronically transfers from your bank account to the business's bank account.

DEPOSIT: to put money into a checking, savings, or other bank account

EXPENSE: something you pay money for

FIXED EXPENSE: an expense that stays basically the same from month to month, such as rent, transportation costs, and tuition

INCOME: money you receive, whether from earnings, gifts, or other sources

INTEREST: money that a borrower pays to a lender for the privilege of borrowing money

LOAN: money given from one person or organization to another with the understanding that the money will be paid back, usually with interest

SAVINGS ACCOUNT: a bank account, usually paying low interest, that does not allow you to write checks

SIMPLE INTEREST: interest paid only on an initial sum of money, with no interest paid on any interest that sum earns

VARIABLE EXPENSES: spending that changes from month to month, such as spending on entertainment and clothing

WITHDRAW: to take money out of a bank account

SELECTED BIBLIOGRAPHY

Bodnar, Janet. *Kiplinger's Dollars and Sense for Kids.* Washington, DC: Kiplinger's Washington Editor, 1999.

Bureau of the Public Debt. *The Savings Bond Owner's Manual.* Washington, DC: Bureau of the Public Debt, U.S. Treasury Department, 2004.

Heady, Robert K., Christy Ottolenghi, and Hugo Ottolenghi. *Complete Idiot's Guide to Managing Your Money.* 4th ed. Indianapolis: Alpha Books, 2001.

Jump$tart Coalition for Personal Financial Literacy, 1997–2011. http://www.jumpstart.org (June 28, 2010).

Miller, J. Steve. *Enjoy Your Money! How to Make It, Save It, Invest It and Give It.* Acworth, GA: Wisdom Creek Press, 2009.

Morris, Kenneth M., and Virginia B. Morris. *Wall Street Journal Guide to Understanding Personal Finance.* New York: Simon Schuster, 2004.

National Endowment for Financial Education. 2011. http://www.nefe.org/ (June 28, 2010).

Shim, Jae K., and Joel G. Siegel. *Budgeting Basics and Beyond.* Hoboken, NJ: John Wiley and Sons, 2008.

Visa. Practical Money Skills for Life, 2000–2011. http://www.practicalmoneyskills.com (June 28, 2010).

FURTHER INFORMATION

Alliance for Investor Education: The Savings Calculator
http://www.investoreducation.org/cindex1.cfm?CFID=4119729&CFTOK
EN=12006957
Check out this cool calculator just for young people. It lets you pick an item
(such as a $5 fast-food meal) and see how much money you'd have in ten
years, twenty years, or at retirement if you skipped the purchase and put
the money into the bank instead.

Butler, Tamsen. *The Complete Guide to Personal Finance: For Teenagers and
College Students*. Ocala, FL: Atlantic Publishing Group, 2010.
Written for teens and young adults, this book focuses on getting and
managing credit, making and sticking to a budget, and determining your
needs versus your wants.

ByDesign Financial Solutions. *Financial Firsts: Your Guide to a Solid Financial
Future*. Los Angeles: ByDesign, 2006.
This financial planning book is for teens and others just beginning to focus
on their finances.

Cardratings.com
http://www.cardratings.com
Compare credit cards and learn more about their various features at this
online clearinghouse of credit card information. The site is hosted by U.S.
Citizens for Fair Credit Card Terms.

CU Succeed
http://www.cusucceed.net/resources.php
Visit this website to find savings calculators; budget worksheets; and lots
of information and articles on credit, savings, and other budgeting topics.

Doeden, Matt. *Shopping Smarts: How to Choose Wisely, Find Bargains, Spot
Swindles, and More*. Minneapolis: Twenty-First Century Books, 2012.
Part of the Teen Wise series, this book tells you how to scout out good deals,
make smart purchasing decisions, handle money and credit wisely, and
protect your rights as a consumer.

Donega, Danielle. *Smart Money: How to Manage Your Cash*. New York: Children's
Press, 2008.
This hip guide tackles the money challenges kids face every day. It includes
cool quizzes, real-life stories, and practical advice.

Donovan, Sandy. *Job Smarts: How to Find Work or Start a Business, Manage Earnings, and More*. Minneapolis: Twenty-First Century Books, 2012.
This guide tells teens how to land a job and keep it and even how to start their own businesses. It offers practical information on searching for a job, writing a résumé, interviewing, and managing your pay.

Gardner, David. *The Motley Fool Investment Guide for Teens: 8 Steps to Having More Money Than Your Parents Ever Dreamed Of*. New York: Fireside, 2002.
Lean all about investing, saving cash, and dodging the financial pitfalls that trap many adults in this fun book from the hosts of National Public Radio's *The Motley Fool*.

Holmberg, Joshua, and David Bruzzese. *The Teen's Guide to Personal Finance: Basic Concepts in Personal Finance That Every Teen Should Know*. Littleton, CO: iUniverse, 2008.
Check out this book that calls itself a "roadmap" to understanding money matters, including banking, interest rates, credit, budget goals, and more.

National Council on Economic Education: It All Adds Up
http://www.italladdsup.org
This fun site is for teens who want to get a head start on their financial futures. You can play online games about saving, investing, buying a car, and other budgeting topics.

National Endowment for Financial Education: My Bread
http://hsfpp.nefe.org/students
This website for high school students has fun activities and articles to help you learn about financial planning, budgeting, debt, and more.

Northwestern Mutual Foundation: The Mint
http://www.themint.org
This website for middle school and high school students has tons of information about creating a budget, investing in the stock market, and more.

PBS Kids: Don't Buy It
http://pbskids.org/dontbuyit
Check out this website to learn how to be "media smart" and how to resist advertising tricks.

Shelley, Susan. *The Complete Idiot's Guide to Money for Teens*. Indianapolis: Alpha Books, 2001.
This easy-to-use reference book has lots of information to help you get a grip on your spending, make sense of bank and credit card statements, and save up for college or a car.

INDEX

ABOUT THE AUTHOR

Sandy Donovan has written several dozen books for kids and teens, including *Job Smarts* and *Scheduling Smarts* for the USA Today Teen Wise Guides series. She has a bachelor's degree in journalism and a master's in public policy and has worked as a newspaper reporter, editor, policy analyst, and website developer. Donovan lives in Minneapolis, Minnesota, with her husband, two sons, and a black lab named Fred. She wrote this book because she's never met a person who regretted having budgeting smarts—and because she hopes her two sons, Henry and Gus, will read it one day.